CRAP CRIMES

Published by Random House Books 2013
2 4 6 8 10 9 7 5 3 1

First published in Great Britain in 2013 by
Random House Books
Random House, 20 Vauxhall Bridge Road,
London SW1V 2SA

www.randomhouse.co.uk

Addresses for companies within The Random House Group Limited can be found at: www.randomhouse.co.uk/offices.htm

The Random House Group Limited Reg. No. 954009

A CIP catalogue record for this book is available from the British Library

ISBN 9781847946935

Designed and produced by
The Curved House/Jim Smith

Printed and bound in China by C&C Offset Printing Co Ltd

INTRODUCTION

As long as there has been crime, there has been 'crap crime'. Look at the Bible – how crap was the stealing of the apple in the Garden of Eden? No alibis, no other suspects, an all-seeing God – it was a bit like smashing a shop window in front of CCTV with no one else around (oh, er – I think we missed that one).

In fact, when you think about it, most criminals are pretty crap, or else we wouldn't know about them. Sure, there exists an echelon of master criminals at the top of the crime chain, too clever to be caught, usually delegating the dirty work to the criminally less well-endowed, but we suspect many of them are just lucky, or maybe pure fiction – Keyser Söze we're looking at you (though not very hard, just in case he really does exist).

Many crimes are also apocryphal – urban myths passed from mouth to mouth, with layer upon layer added until the original, mundane offence bears little or no resemblance to the masterminded act of deceit, cunning and derring-do which has Inspector Foiled of the Yard scratching his head in wonderment and barely disguised admiration.

CRAP CRIMES

Martin & Simon Toseland

The internet is full of such stories – reported crimes which have their origins in musty newspaper reports and police logs but which, through the agency of websites, repetitions and what used to be called 'Chinese whispers', have become more fanciful, more outlandish and more impressive.

HOW TO COMMIT A CRAP CRIME

- **Be a stupid criminal** – a diminal. Essential if the crime is to be truly crap.
- **Don't plan** – 'plan for success' is an expression that would leave most diminals scratching their heads.
- **Overestimate your own criminal cunning** – a little self-knowledge would have prevented most of these offences occurring.
- **Abuse alcohol and/or drugs** – to be sure of really messing things up, it helps to execute your crime while barely able to stand or speak.
- **Bad timing** – just to ensure you enter the hallowed halls of crapness, carry out your crime while some police officers happen to be strolling by.

Our little book records some of these crimes – which often cross the border between factual reportage and urban legend – but it also contains many crimes which appear to be exaggerated or fictional (but actually aren't) simply because it is difficult to believe anyone could have been so stupid. It is almost as if the perpetrators of some of these offences have been raised on urban myths and decided that's the way to commit a robbery or plan a heist.

There is a plottable correlation, we've decided, between the crapness of the crime and the intoxication of the criminal. On a graph it might run: X Axis – mistimed jump, handbrake left off, forgot gun, went to wrong bank; Y Axis – slightly tiddly, ratted, mashed, criminally incapable.

There is a term for this kind of incompetence – the Dunning–Kruger effect. This syndrome was reported by psychologists David Dunning and Justin Kruger in the late 1990s. They found that if a group of people was asked to assess their own performance at a task, the worst performers were also the worst at measuring their own proficiency: to put it another way, they had an inflated opinion of their own ability.

The Dunning–Kruger effect can be found in the bucketload on most of these pages – people boasting of their own crimes on Facebook, or calling the police to complain about being short-sold cocaine – but mostly in the utter failure to anticipate the most rudimentary obstacles to success in their chosen career. In short, being crap criminals. Without them this book would not exist – but we can't really thank them.

Please note that names and details of many of the crimes in this book have been changed to protect the identities of the criminally stupid. After all, everyone deserves a second chance, right?
Ok, a twentieth chance then.

MARTIN & SIMON TOSELAND
June 2013

TOP TEN CRAP CRIMES

In a book full of crap crime, here is the crème de la pooh.

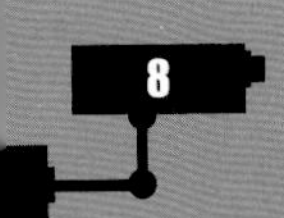

ROBBERY WITH POOR DRAWING SKILLS

Matthew McNelly and Joey Miller were arrested by police in 2009 when their disguises failed to pass muster. Unable to find balaclavas to hide their identities, they improvised by drawing masks on their faces with a black permanent marker pen. Having successfully pulled off a burglary the unlucky pair were spotted by a bystander as they broke into the 'getaway' car. (Yes, every detail of the robbery was meticulously planned.) The witness described the ingenious robbers as having 'painted faces' and also gave a description of the car.

When the police caught up with the stolen car moments later they found that the men had their ingeniously idiotic disguises still in place. They were both charged with second-degree burglary and, in what might go some way to explaining the story, McNelly was given a further charge of drink driving. Neither has an art qualification.

STUPIDITY SENTENCE Life and extra art classes.

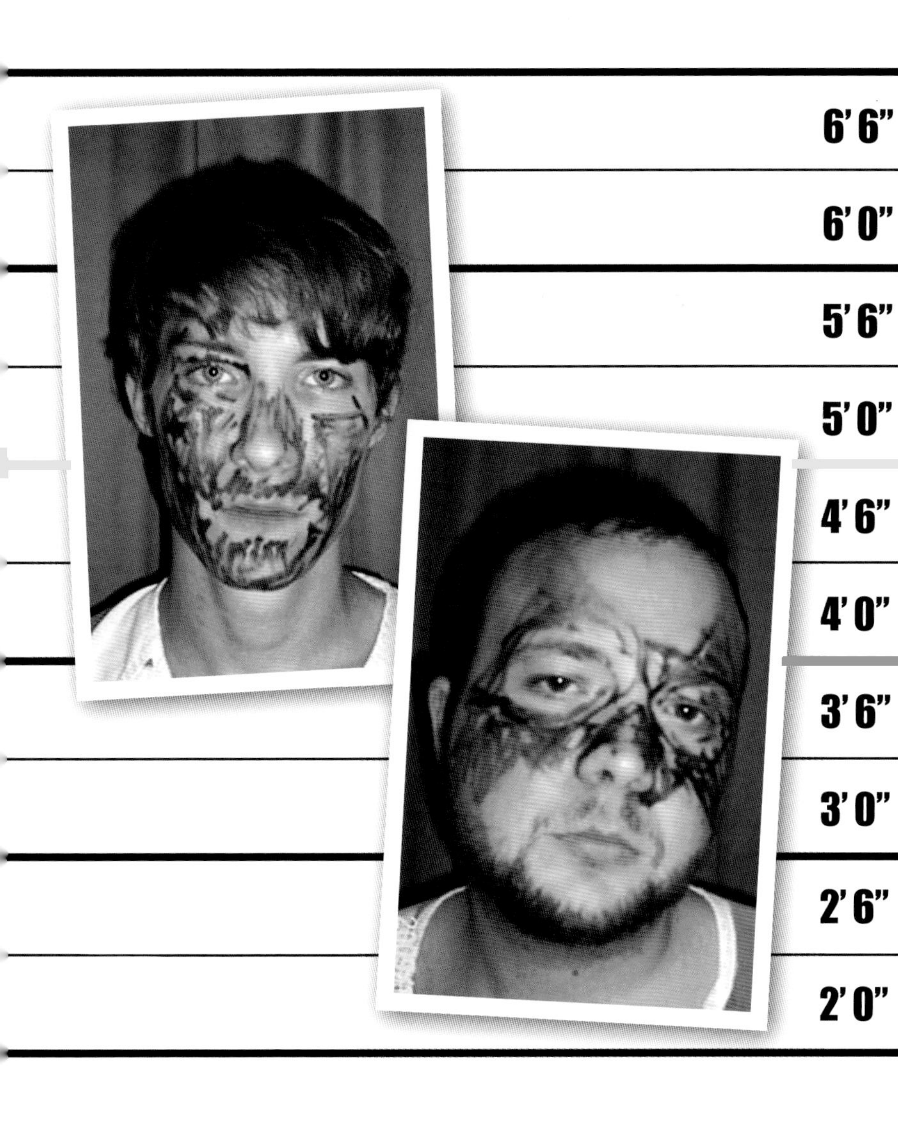
6' 6"
6' 0"
5' 6"
5' 0"
4' 6"
4' 0"
3' 6"
3' 0"
2' 6"
2' 0"

ESCAPE FAIL

Two Californian teenagers, who were caught in the act of breaking into a car, saved everyone a lot of trouble when they scaled a fence while trying to evade chasing policemen. One of the officers explained: ‘People just don’t break into prison everyday, let alone the notorious San Quentin penitentiary.’

TEENAGE ROBBER FAILS TO DELIVER

A suspected robber had to be freed by fire crews after a police patrol caught him with his arm stuck in the letterbox of a house in Colchester. The 17-year-old boy was found by police on the doorstep of the property at around three o'clock on a Wednesday morning.

Fire crews were called to the scene to remove the letterbox – which remained attached to the teenager's arm – from the door. He was arrested and taken to the police station, where the letterbox was removed.

The homeowner was not in the house at the time. She said that when police talked to the youth, he said he was trying to find a party and thought it was at this house. They had seen the boy on his knees, banging the door, and assumed that he had just got stuck. Later they realised he was trying to get into the house through the letterbox.

She continued: 'At first I was upset but when I thought about it I laughed. To think he tried to get in through that little letterbox.'

Her daughter said the area is normally very quiet. Police charged the foolish felon with attempted burglary (in letterbox format).

LETTERS

DRUNK IN CHARGE OF A SPELLCHECKER

When smuggling cheap plonk from Asia and attempting to pass it off as a well-known brand, it's a good idea to make the labelling look convincing.

Surrey County Council Trading Standards issued a warning to drinkers after hundreds of bottles of fake Jacob's Creek wine were seized in the region. The counterfeit booze was rumbled because it was selling for about £2 a bottle – way below the price for the genuine wine – and it tasted foul. The other big clue was the label on the back claiming it was a 'Wine from Austrlia' – even 'Oz' would have been more convincing.

STUPIDITY SENTENCE A hundred lines: 'I mustn't blunder when I spell "Down Under".'

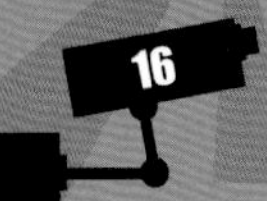

SEE-THROUGH CRIME

A bank, a wizard and an idiot should never be mixed, is the lesson from this less-than-magical crime.

A man was quickly overpowered by queuing customers in an Iranian bank when he started snatching cash from their hands.

'I made a mistake. I understand now what a big trick was played on me,' the man later told the court, after being charged with attempted robbery. He explained that he had paid 5 million rials (nearly £300) to a 'wizard' for spells which, when tied to his arms, would render the would-be thief invisible, allowing him to rob a bank while scaring the living daylights out of staff and customers alike. Perhaps testing his newly acquired cloak of invisibility before entering the bank would have been a good idea. But then perhaps not believing the wizard in the first place would have been a better precaution. Either way, only one of them disappeared with the cash.

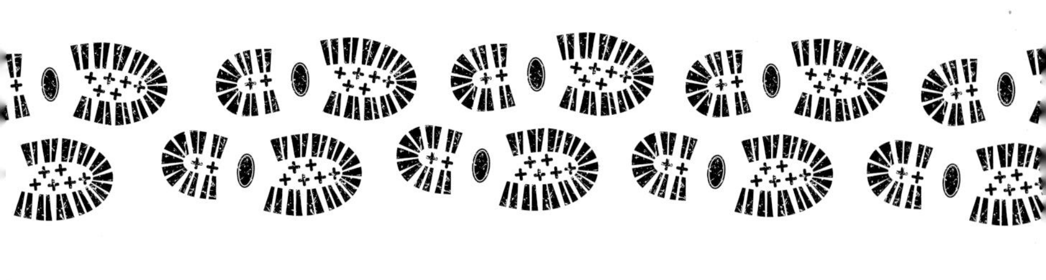

CRACK, BACK AND ?

A woman from North Carolina saw her attempt to enlist the force of the law in her cause badly misfire on her.

The woman, aged 50, approached a police officer in the parking lot of a convenience store, and complained that she'd been sold some poor-quality crack cocaine and wanted her money back.

As proof she took the crack out of her mouth, placing it on the trunk of the officer's squad car.

The deputy warned her that, if the substance tested positive, she would be arrested. It did, and she was.

To make things worse, the man she accused of selling her the inferior drugs was searched by police, who found nothing on him.

LARCENY LESSON Never take illegal goods to the police unless you're sure they're corrupt.

Drugs

DUMMER AND DUMMKOPF

Two German men in their twenties stopped to ask a police patrol for directions to the Czech Republic. Something in their manner must have made the police suspicious, or maybe it was a large bag marked 'SWAG' on the back seat of their car.

In any event, officers searched the vehicle, found what appeared to be stolen goods and arrested the pair. The men later admitted breaking into three car dealerships. Pity they didn't steal a sat nav while they were there.

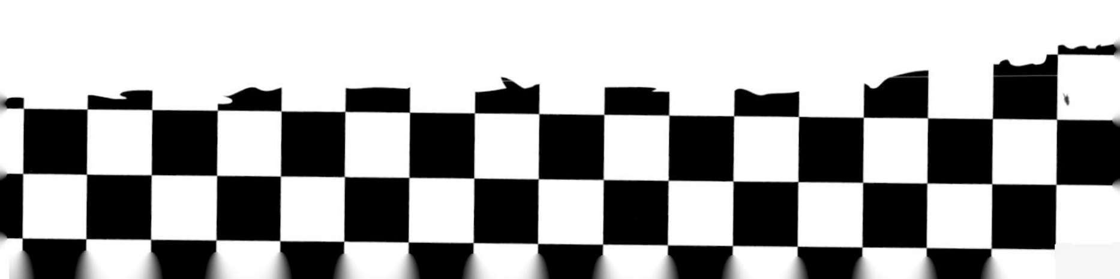

NEEDS OF HIS OWN

A 55-year-old Chicago teacher, Arthur Jennings, who had taught special-needs students for twenty years, was hauled to the headteacher's office to explain his appalling attendance record, which included missing over 30 days in a year. Not bad when you think about teachers' holidays!

Unfortunately that's when Jennings had the great idea which propelled him into the august ranks of the criminally crap.

He figured that by laying his hands on a stolen doctor's prescription pad he could concoct an excuse so convincing that his absence would never be questioned again and his job would remain safe.

He came up with: 'I am a coke addict.' It probably wasn't the best excuse the judge had heard – he sentenced Jennings to a year in jail for forgery – but it must have made him chuckle.

STUPIDITY SENTENCE Make sure anything you write on a doctor's prescription pad is illegible, especially if it's incriminating.

Rx

PATIENT NAME:

ADDRESS:

DIRECTIONS:

SIGNATURE:

DATE:

CRIMINAL DISPLAY

Every child knows that when you light the blue touchpaper you need to stand back. Unfortunately 'Gary Forks' wasn't a child – he was a crap criminal from Wisconsin. So when he decided to hold up a store selling fireworks, he ignored the entire Firework Safety Code and, in an attempt to intimidate the owner, fired a warning shot from his shotgun into a stack of Roman candles. In the ensuing whizzbang chaos, it was the would-be felon who lost his nerve and fled the store, running straight into the arms of the police officers who had arrived to check out the fine display of fireworks prematurely lighting up the neighbourhood.

VERDICT Leave crime to the bright sparks.

THEY RATTED ON US . . .

In Manila, a remarkable dispute arose over how secure the police evidence room was after more than half a ton of marijuana, cocaine and amphetamines went missing. The chief called a press conference to quash rumours over the integrity of the police officers themselves.

'How dare you accuse us of theft,' he raged. 'Clearly shoddy workmanship is the culprit here. Rats and cockroaches got in through gaps in the locker doors and ate it all, every last scrap.' As conclusive proof of the vermin's guilt he pointed out that the cockroaches had been behaving 'very oddly. They just stand there looking dazed when we shine a light on them . . . obviously they have been getting high on drugs.'

Case closed. Or it was until a reporter at the press conference produced pictures of officers selling the drugs at an outdoor market near to the station.

STUCK ON GLUE

Addicts can meet very sticky ends – particularly if their substance of choice is adhesive. One such sniffer found his way one Saturday night into the factory of what he described as the *premier cru* of glues – Gola Gola Quickstix – in Belo Horizonte, Brazil. Unable to control himself, he filled his lungs directly from one of the huge open vats on the factory floor. Unfortunately, the hit was so good that he knocked over the tank as he reeled away. When he woke from his sticky reverie, he thought with horror that he had become paralysed from the strength of the drug – but in fact his entire body, not just his clothes, was stuck fast to the factory floor.

When workers arrived at the factory on Monday morning, they called the emergency services. The fire brigade had to use power saws to cut around him, removing twelve planks of wood as well as the unfortunate glue-sniffer. Despite literally losing the skin off his back when the wood was finally pared from him, he maintained it was all worth it. The local police chief was less than sympathetic. 'What is it with these people?' he asked. 'Are they nuts?'

POLICE LINE DO NOT CROSS POLICE LINE
DO NOT CROSS POLICE LINE
CROSS POLICE LINE DO NOT CROSS
DO NOT CROSS POLICE LINE DO NOT

WOULD YOU LIKE THAT IN LARGE DENOMINATIONS, SIR?

A young man walks into a bank, waits in line and then hands the teller a cheque to cash. An everyday occurrence. In this case, the teller was moved to press the little red button when she read the amount. 26-year-old Ray Johnson hoped to walk out of the bank with a cool $360 billion. He claimed, when questioned, that his girlfriend's mother had given him the cheque to help start up a record business. EMI perhaps? The generous sponsor denied having written the cheque or given Johnson permission to use her cheque book. When our crap criminal turned out his pocket a small amount of cannabis was discovered – you can't help wondering how much he'd used before he walked into the bank.

VERDICT Stupidity on a bank-breaking scale.

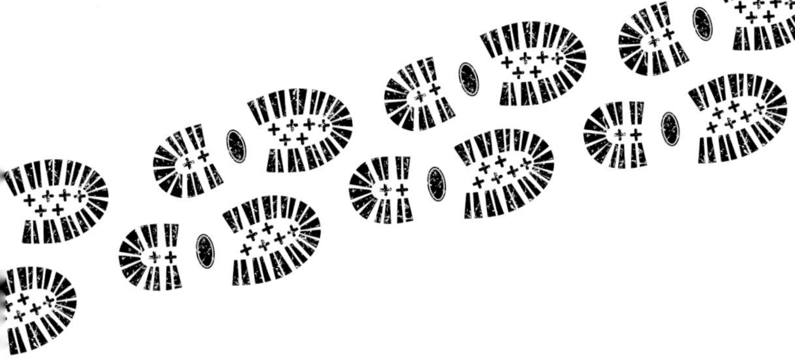

MURDER, HE WROTE

When Polish writer Krystian Bala finally got his first novel, *Amok*, published in 2003, it made little impact on the general reading public. This was until police, investigating the murder of a Polish small-business owner in 2000, became suspicious of Bala. Deciding to give his book a thumb through, they were immediately struck by similarities between the murder in the novel and the actual crime. The author had included details in his 'fictional' account of the crime that only the real-life murderer could have known. In 2007, Bala was sentenced to jail for 25 years for planning and committing the murder. Sales of *Amok* went through the roof. Bala is now working on his second novel, although the police may have to edit the story – they found details on his computer for plans to kill a second victim to tie in with the plot. This might affect Bala's final sentence.

TRUE CRIME TIP Don't take 'write what you know' too literally.

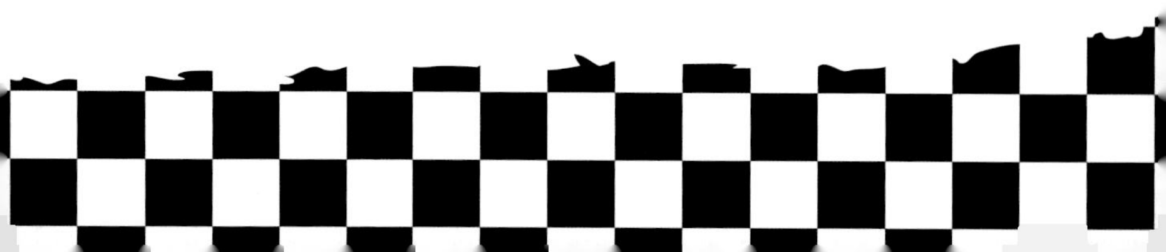

HOOKED ON CRIME

If you're going to steal your best friend and neighbour's fishing rods, it's probably best not to try and pawn them in the same town. Admittedly Artie McBass got unlucky when he opened the door of the pawn shop to find said friend, Ernie Ford, having a pleasant conversation with the owner. It took seconds for Ford to notice that McBass was holding his fishing rods, which had gone missing from his garage that very same morning. McBass attempted to explain that he'd just borrowed the rods, but his panicked expression wasn't convincing Ford or the pawn shop owner. He turned and fled from the shop like a pilchard fleeing a whale. The police caught him soon enough. 'There was always something fishy about him,' Ernie should have thought to himself. 'Maybe he was looking for a prawn shop?'

DETENTION FOR BEING STUPID

A man in Anchorage, Alaska, had left his car outside with the engine running to try and warm it up before starting the journey to work on a cold winter's morning. Having packed his lunch and readied himself, he left his house only to find the car had disappeared.

It didn't take long for a police patrol to find the car parked just a few streets away – right outside the local high school. 'Surely not,' they thought. 'Even school age criminals must have learned the basics of crime.' Just in case they were wrong, an officer waited within sight of the stolen vehicle as a bell signalled the end of the school day. He was almost disappointed when three teenage boys came running out of the building and jumped straight in the car. The boys were easily apprehended though not, one sadly suspects, for the final time in their lives.

CRIMINAL HOMEWORK A hundred lines: 'I will not shit on my own doorstep.'

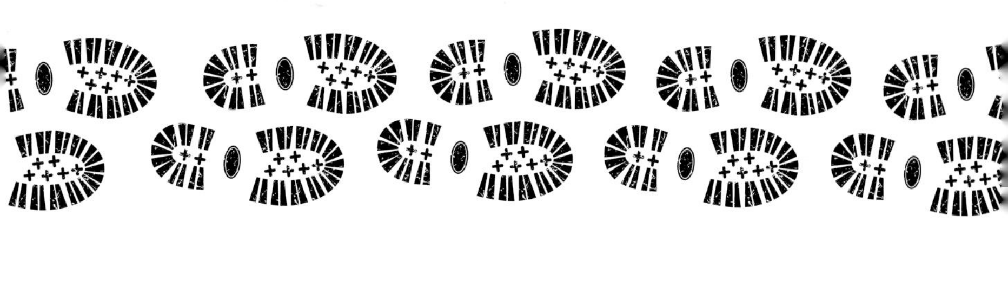

MyCrime

Bragging about your crimes is never smart; bragging about them on social media sites is even less smart. But we're going to need a whole new category of 'not smart' to describe taunting the police when they are on to you. Some might say that if you're going to do this, then MySpace is probably the best place to do it, but not Minneapolis criminal Courtney Martin; not anymore. Martin was wanted by police for passing fraudulent cheques in several cities when, via her MySpace account, she invited Officer Kronsky to 'Go fuck yourself. You ain't never gonna catch me officer dipshit.'

STATUS UPDATE She was wrong.

THE BLIND DOG ASSASSIN

'Lucky is basically a damn good guide dog,' said his trainer. 'He just needs a little brush up on some elementary skills.'

The evidence, though, points in the opposite direction, just as Lucky should have done when he guided his first blind owner to her death by walking out in front of a moving bus. And, in fact, when he led his second owner over the edge of a pier and to his death. It might just have been possible to blame extreme bad luck for Lucky's strike rate – two owners, two full coffins. Things took a nasty turn, though, when the canine Capone pushed his third owner into the path of an express train. He topped his murderous spree off by guiding his fourth and final victim to the middle of a very busy road before abandoning her and making his escape. Lucky is not how you'd describe his next owner.

VERDICT The unkind leading the blind.

UNLIKELY TO OFFEND

Most of us have a clear idea of when we might be breaking the law, but sometimes it's wise to expect the unexpected (even if you're engaged in a pretty odd but harmless activity).

Here are some of the more arresting arrestable offences.

- It is illegal to whale-watch in landlocked Utah.
- It is illegal for a man to wear a spaghetti strap dress in Miami.
- It is illegal to cross the road while walking on your hands in Connecticut.
- It is illegal to name your pig Napoleon in France.
- It is illegal to enter London's House of Commons in a suit of armour.
- It is illegal to die in the House of Commons.

Genuine criminal geniuses plan their crimes meticulously. At the heart of such planning is identifying a suitably vulnerable target. Top of that list would not normally be a shop that supplies CCTV cameras. That did not stop one aspiring master of crime, Steven Dawes, who broke in to Central Cameras one night. Each of his precisely planned moves – smashing the front door, trying to pick up various computers only to find them bolted to the shelves – was caught on at least twelve of the cameras prominently displayed around the shop. Dawes seems to have remembered at this point that his actions might be being recorded, as he pulled his hood over his head to disguise himself, but only having peered closely into the lens of each of the cameras. Finally our modern-day Dillinger grabbed $250 from the till and made his well-rehearsed escape. Sadly his hiding place, behind a bush outside the shop, was also picked up on film and police apprehended him as soon as they arrived on the scene.

ILLEGAL DUMPING

In a crime that could have inspired the title of this book, a 48-year-old man was charged with littering – or rather dumping – after he was caught doing a number two in a retired police officer's driveway. The dumper offered up a full confession and a bizarre excuse. He explained that he goes running at 4 am every day and, at about the two-mile mark, feels the need to evacuate. So wherever he is at the time becomes his very own Portaloo. The retired police officer became suspicious after finding seven 'calling cards' and installed video surveillance equipment to catch the perpetrator. Our friend was caught in *craprante delicto* and charged by police.

VERDICT Crap crime.

WHO NEEDS LEGAL AID?

Appearing in court on the charge of stealing a car, a defendant was asked by the judge, 'How do you plead?' Rather than going with the usual, 'Not guilty, yer 'onour', the man responded with: 'Let me explain why I stole the car.' While the man's lawyer went for a 'facepalm' response, the judge ruled the case and moved on.

STUPIDITY SENTENCE Why pay a lawyer when you can find yourself guilty?

DA DA DA DA DA (NOT) BATMAN!

A Michigan man dressed as Batman was arrested for obstruction of a police investigation. Officers arrived at the scene of a traffic accident to find that the driver responsible for the crash had absconded. They decided to use trained police dogs to search the area for him, which is when they encountered the caped crusader, who had taken it upon himself to assist in the search.

According to a court affidavit the legendary crime fighter, who had learned of the accident by monitoring police radio, claimed he had 'just happened' to be wearing the costume when he turned up to help search the area. The police asked him to leave, as his scent might mislead the dogs. When he refused, they arrested him.

In fact, the batty Batman had been arrested on a previous occasion, when police found him in costume on the roof of a local business, armed with a collapsible baton and a pepper spray in his 'utility belt'.

VERDICT Super zero.

POLICE LINE DO NOT CROSS POLICE LINE
DO NOT CROSS POLICE LINE
DO NOT CROSS POLICE LINE

BAG THE EVIDENCE

It seems that trying to bluff your way out of a misdemeanour isn't just restricted to 'ordinary' people. The instinct to try to get away with it sits in the DNA of the rich and famous too – even though their high-visibility lives mean the chances of them doing so are even slimmer. Consider Paris Hilton, who was was arrested for possession of cocaine. The police noticed a small packet of white powder fall out of a bag she was carrying. The heiress initially claimed that the substance was chewing gum. When that excuse, surprisingly, didn't wash with the police, she denied it was her bag until a picture was produced showing her holding the selfsame bag, at which point not even the most creative PR could make the accusation go away.

OLICE LINE DO NOT CROSS POLICE LINE DO NOT C

PISS-POOR DESIGNER BRIEFS

Tom Sizemore – he of *Saving Private Ryan* fame – offered a branded alibi when accused in court of attempting to falsify a urine test. The police claimed that Sizemore had used a prosthetic penis called 'The Whizzinator' sewn into his underwear to produce the sample. The device comes equipped with dried urine, a syringe and heater packs (to keep the urine at body temperature). When confronted with the underwear and device in court, Sizemore came up with a piss-poor excuse: 'They're not mine. They're Calvins. I wear Hilfigers.' He was sentenced to both jail and rehab for violating his probation.

STERILE
TIGHTEN CAP SECURELY
APRIETE TAPA CON SEGURIDAD
BIEN FERMER LE BOUCHON
After Use: May Contain Hazardous Materials
Des Pues de Uso: Puede Contener Materiales Peligrosos
Après Usage: Peut Contenir Matieres Dangereuses
Name
Nombre
Nom:
F/M
M/H:
Fecha
Date:

REPEAT AFTER ME...

Police in Mexico City asked each man in a line-up of robbery suspects to repeat the words 'Give me your money or I'll shoot you.' They were astonished when the first man protested, 'but that's not what I said!'

LARCENY LESSON Learn your lines.

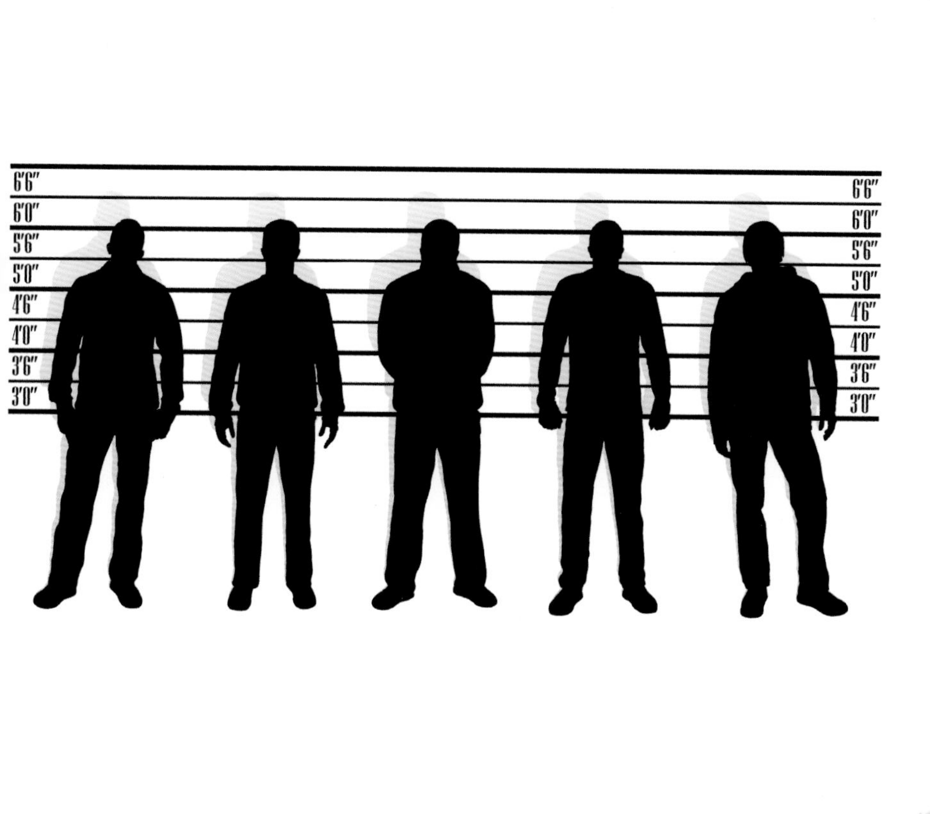
6'6"
6'0"
5'6"
5'0"
4'6"
4'0"
3'6"
3'0"

ROBBERY NOT ON THE MENU

A would-be felon in Houston walked into a Burger King at 7.50 am, showed a gun to the server and demanded that she hand over all the cash. The young woman stared at him blankly and said she couldn't open the till without a food order. He thought for a minute and ordered his favourite – onion rings. 'We don't serve those for breakfast, sir,' she responded, at which point the McThief decided to take his order elsewhere.

LARCENY LESSON Don't attempt robbery on an empty stomach.

PANIC ATTACK

It seems that it's not uncommon for police officers all over the world to take some extra remuneration in the course of their jobs. The little extra can be in the form of cash, perks or making use of the spoils of others' misdemeanours. A Mexican police officer recently availed himself of a small quantity of marijuana confiscated from an offender. He and his wife made some, er, cakes. So far, so normal. Things started to go wrong, though, when both husband and wife started to feel very bad. In a completely stoned panic, the officer rang the emergency services, confessed all and pleaded for help. 'I think we're dying. We made brownies and we're dying, I really think we're dead.'

DON'T SAY Watch out, the cookie monster is behind you.

THE FOURTH WALL

Crap criminals in Scotland spent fifteen minutes carefully picking the lock of an attractive cottage door. Imagine their surprise when, on finally breaking and entering the premises, they were met with stunning views of the local countryside – through an empty building. Not only were the owners not in, but the cupboards, had there been any, would have been totally bare.

The cottage was a three-sided film prop constructed for a local TV company, and the would-be burglars' every move was caught on a nearby security camera. Definitely a case of check around the back before going in the front.

CRIME AGAINST SANITARY

'Mr Strong is a man of considerable intellectual ability, but there has been a clear problem over the past year relating to drug abuse, which heightened his fascination with alchemy, and with turning base matter into gold . . .' So said the defence barrister after Mr Strong had been accused of arson and endangering the lives of others.

The base matter in this case was his own faeces. In the course of the year he became convinced he could turn it into gold simply by drying his natural waste on an electric heater. The prosecuting barrister summed up what happened next:

'Unfortunately you failed to recognise that faeces naturally turns into fuel as it dries out, not into metal, and your actions created a fire that caused £3,000 worth of damage to the block of flats . . . in which you reside.'

Sentencing the accused to three months in jail, the judge observed he'd heard of Fool's Gold but this was the first time he'd come across Stool's Gold.

TOO MUCH INFORMATION

Some people, particularly those of a criminal bent, think you have to be pretty stupid to be a police informant, and James Tynan, occasional stool pigeon for a small-town American police department, seemed intent on proving them right.

One sunny afternoon Tynan walked into the police station and, using his knowledge of the building from previous visits, headed straight for the evidence room, where he purloined $1,000 in tainted banknotes before making his way out.

This, however, was only step one of his masterful heist. On the way home, he realised that his fingerprints would be all over the cop shop, as he had not had the foresight to wear gloves, so he returned to wipe down all the surfaces he could recall touching. Phew!

Except, astonishingly to Tynan there were security cameras recording every last second of his bungled burglary and, of course, the local force quickly recognised him as an informant. The chief of police scratched his head, calling Tynan 'one of America's dumbest criminals', a sure sign that a life of crime isn't, perhaps, the life for you.

A CRIME AGAINST MUSIC

Judges on shows like *American Idol* and *The X Factor* are expected to offer constructive criticism, no matter how challenging this may be.

But if you're a karaoke singer in a Baltimore bar, perhaps you shouldn't assume the same level of professional behaviour from your audience, and should check them out before demanding feedback. This would have been useful advice for 22-year-old Crystal Rogers, whose extraordinary rendition of Whitney Houston's 'I Will Always Love You' provoked some hostile heckling from a group of Whitney fans in the room.

Ideally this would have been the moment that Crystal took a bow and gracefully withdrew from the stage, instead of asking the 'm*therf*ckers' what was wrong.

The six lovely ladies decided to impose their own interpretation of boot camp on poor Crystal, who quickly found herself in need of a bodyguard, and on the wrong end of a karaoke-inspired kicking. The 'judges' were arrested on assault charges – probably the only way any of them will make it onto our TV screens in the future.

SOME LIKE IT HOT

After falling out with his wife one time too many, one 42-year-old man thought he'd express the depth of his anger by destroying a treasured possession of hers. Did he take a chainsaw to her wardrobe? No. Take her beloved chihuahua to the dog pound? Uh-uh. He decided to do a one-man demolition job on her car. Well, their car. So far, so dumb.

He set about the vehicle with relish, battering the windscreen and doors with a sledgehammer. But, stepping back to admire his handiwork, the furious husband decided he hadn't really made his point, and so came to the course of action that gained him entry to the august ranks of the criminally crap. He doused the car with petrol – inside and out – and then sat in the driver's seat to set it alight.

Even instantly realising his mistake wasn't enough to save him from first-degree burns, an arson charge and a demand for a divorce.

CRAP ADVICE You're only supposed to blow the bloody doors off!

DO NOT CROSS POLICE LINE DO NOT CROSS

POLICE LINE DO NOT CROSS POLICE LINE DO NOT

CAR TROUBLE

One morning Dan Fleckle found that his Corvette had a flat battery. He jump-started the car and returned the jump leads to the garage, leaving the motor running and the driver's door open. While he was away an opportunistic thief slipped into the car, locked the doors, closed the electric windows and attempted to reverse down the drive.

Sadly, though, the thief didn't know how to drive a manual car and stalled. He attempted to restart the engine but the battery was flat. In short, he had imprisoned himself. The police constable called to the incident described what happened next:

'The owner called 911, and waited for us to arrive. Meanwhile, the thief tried to break the Corvette's window with the owner's steering lock, but was not successful. He then attempted to smash it with a hatchet he carried in his backpack, but still couldn't break out. By the time we arrived, he had finally smashed a window and was attempting to crawl through the gap. After we arrested him, we showed him that all he'd needed to do to escape was to manually unlock the door by sliding the lock button.'

DO NOT CROSS POLICE LINE DO NOT CROSS

POLICE LINE DO NOT CROSS POLICE LINE

REPRIEVED BY BOREDOM

'You're guilty, I'm certain of that, but I simply can't bear to listen to your damned accountant any longer,' an emotional judge announced in Ottawa. The trial was about an insurance company which had been accused of multiple counts of tax evasion. The judge justified her decision to dismiss the case: 'It is my observation that your accountant is beyond a doubt the dullest witness I've ever had in my court. He speaks in a monotonal voice so totally devoid of interest, and uses language so drab and convoluted, that even the court reporter cannot stay conscious long enough to record his evidence properly. Three solid days of his steady drone as he defends an obviously fraudulent set of end-of-year accounts is enough. I cannot face the prospect of another fourteen indictments. It's probably unethical but I don't care. Case dismissed.'

TO ALL CRAP CRIMINALS Make sure you employ this accountant regardless of your crime.

There are times when you simply have to confess. A failed businessman with a bad drug habit ran into a local newsagent in Powys in an attempt to hold it up. He threatened the shop owner with a knife, demanding that the contents of the till be handed over. When the brave newsagent refused, there was a struggle in which the robber's mask was ripped from his face. However, the robber managed to escape with the cash drawer from the till. He ran from the shop and to his nearby home. Unfortunately the drawer opened as he left the shop, leaving a trail of banknotes leading straight to his door.

When police officers arrived at his house he opened the door and confessed immediately. In a rare example of legal humour, his lawyer summed up the case nicely: 'He made a hash of his life.'

ADVICE TO POLICE Always follow the money.

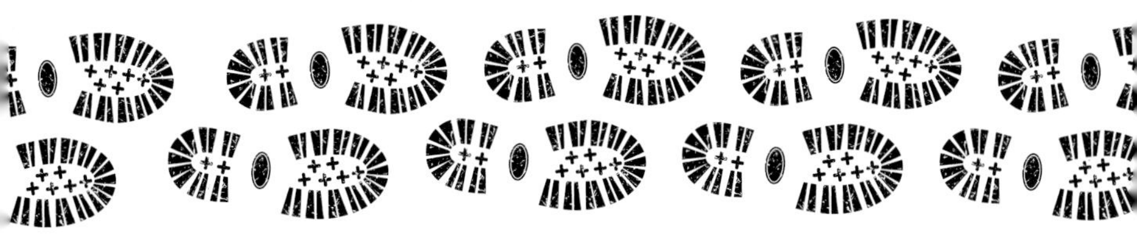

WHO'S GOING TO DRIVE YOU HOME?

A 50-year-old mobile DJ from Yorkshire was branded 'Britain's worst driver' after clocking up a staggering 59 driving bans, and a total of 110 driving offences.

He was eventually jailed after being caught driving a van with no insurance, while disqualified, three days before he was due to be sentenced for another crime.

The DJ was rendered temporarily immobile with a jail sentence of five months. His solicitor said he was a victim of poor decision-making.

IDIOT
DRIVERS

Next
15 miles

DRIVEN TO DRINK?

A British motorist was jailed after 'staggering' out of his car and being found to be four times over the legal alcohol limit when stopped by police. He was still disqualified from a previous ban at the time. It was his tenth drink driving offence. In addition he had accumulated another 50 driving offences in 30 years, including 28 instances of driving while disqualified and without insurance.

According to his solicitor, the latest offence had occurred after he had heard that his wife was seeing another man. He had got in the car, which he claimed he had bought as a present for his wife, and driven to their house where his fears were confirmed.

He was described by the magistrate as being like 'a loaded gun on the road'.

NOT KEYSER SÖZE

The identity of Ireland's worst driver was discovered by a diligent cop, who was puzzled why the multiple offender had not been apprehended for his reckless behaviour.

Prawo Jazdy had had his licence details recorded over 50 times by Garda traffic police, but it appeared the criminal mastermind had as many addresses as speeding and parking violations to his name.

That was until the bright officer realised that 'Prawo Jazdy' was actually the Polish for 'Driving Licence' – not the name of an unsettled European felon. The Garda are still on the hunt for Ridičský Průkaz and Carta De Condução, thought to be from the Czech Republic and Portugal respectively.

PL

DO YOU HAVE A WHEELBARROW FOR THE CHANGE, SIR?

A Jacksonville man walked into a hypermarket, browsed the aisles for a while, and put a microwave, a hoover and a few other things into his trolley. He sauntered to the checkout and handed over a $1 million bill to pay for the $483 worth of goods. Unsurprisingly the person on checkout queried the validity of the note. The customer insisted that it was legal tender. Unconvinced, the assistant called the hypermarket manager, who called the police. All the while, the customer insisted that the note was genuine. It wasn't. He was arrested and charged with attempting to purchase goods under false pretences.

1,000,000
FEDERAL RESERVE NOTE
AB 81511921 S
B2
M 54
1,000,000
NON-NEGOTIABLE
ONE
MILLION
THIS NOTE IS NOT LEGAL TENDER
FOR ANY DEBTS, PUBLIC OR PRIVATE
Treasurer of Conmar Corporation
M 1
AB 81511921 S
JEFFERSON
SERIES
1996
1,000,000
THE
UNITED STATES OF AMERICA
ONE MILLION
Secretary of the Treasurer
1,000,000

SMOKED OUT...

Insurance companies now pride themselves on their rigorous assessment of claims, and potential fraudsters should be wary of taking them on. So it proved for a cigar fan in Kentucky. He bought a very expensive box of 24 rare finest Havanas and insured them against, among other things, fire. Within a month, however, he found the allure of the cigars too much and had smoked the whole box without having even paid the first instalment on his insurance policy. In his claim the cunning cigarist said that the cigars had all been lost in a series of small fires. A sceptical judge upheld his claim and the insurance company paid up $15,000 rather than go through a costly legal battle.

However, as soon as the smoking fraudster banked the cheque, the insurance company had him arrested on 24 counts of arson – using his own insurance claim and testimony as evidence. Our sly smoker emerged from jail 24 months later, and $24,000 poorer.

RISK PROFILE Uninsurable.

GIVING THE AUTHORITIES THE FINGER

A dentist from South Carolina and two brothers cooked up a painful scam. The dentist allowed the brothers to chop off one of his fingers with a hatchet so that they could claim on their household accident policy. The dentist also claimed on his disability policy. The three men got lucky on both claims and the dentist used some of the money to buy a yacht, which he rather hubristically called *Minus One*. The authorities became suspicious and charged the men. Perhaps the dentist's yacht should be rechristened *Oops*, as the men are all spending time in the clink.

POLICE LINE DO NOT CROSS POLICE LINE DO NOT
POLICE LINE DO NOT CROSS POLICE LINE DO NOT
DO NOT CROSS POLICE LINE DO NOT CROSS

SMOKING IS BAD FOR YOU

A robber in Utah clearly hadn't watched enough movie car chases before committing his crime. Otherwise why, with police helicopters following him and directing squad cars to his location, would he have suddenly stopped at a convenience store and politely bought a pack of cigarettes, not stopping to collect the change but giving his pursuers time to catch up? And what is the point of robbing a business and then squandering your ill-gotten gains on fags anyway?

Needless to say he was caught soon after, before he'd even had a chance to unwrap the packet.

TANGOED WITH CASH

A Texan bank robber escaped with a holdall of money, but made the mistake of opening a packet of the dollar bills – which had been booby-trapped with a dye bomb – outside. He was covered in orange paint but instead of fleeing he threw away the tainted notes, used a public toilet to change into his getaway clothes, and then sauntered back to a bus stop outside of the very bank he had robbed, to calmly wait for his bus. Unsurprisingly the police got there first and arrested him – his dyed orange face and hands were a bit of a giveaway.

STATES
275622L
100
DOLLARS

NOT A HAPPY MEAL

A small-time Miami crook placed his order at a drive-thru burger restaurant. The server told him that his bill would be $10.83, but the man responded that he could only pay $2.50 – that's all he had on him. Upon hearing that this wouldn't do and his order had been cancelled, the crook got out of his car, walked to the cashier's window, pulled a gun and demanded his food. When the brave cashier refused, the man grabbed a handful of ketchup sachets in a bid to save face. On the way back to his car, perhaps realising the stupidity of his crime, he even ditched the red sauce. A passing police car prevented his escape.

DO NOT CROSS POLICE LINE DO NOT CROSS
Ketchup

CHIPS MIT DEM?

A Munich man, somewhat off his trolley, tried to rob a bank armed with a water pistol and a potato peeler. 55-year-old Gunther Müller at least had the sense to wear a stocking over his head – perhaps it muffled the sniggering of the unimpressed cashier who, not intimidated by his weapons, told him the bank had run out of cash.

'Mr Potato Head' was arrested shortly afterwards, still wearing the stocking.

STUPIDITY SENTENCE If at first you don't succeed, fry, fry, fry again.

CHARGE OF STUPIDITY

A dumb New York burglar gave new meaning to the term 'smartphone' when he left his on charge during a robbery. He was disturbed at the scene and fled, leaving his mobile plugged in.

Police called one of his contacts, saying the phone's owner had been involved in an accident, and asked for his contact details so they could inform the family. The 23-year-old felon was arrested for breaking and entering, though not for battery.

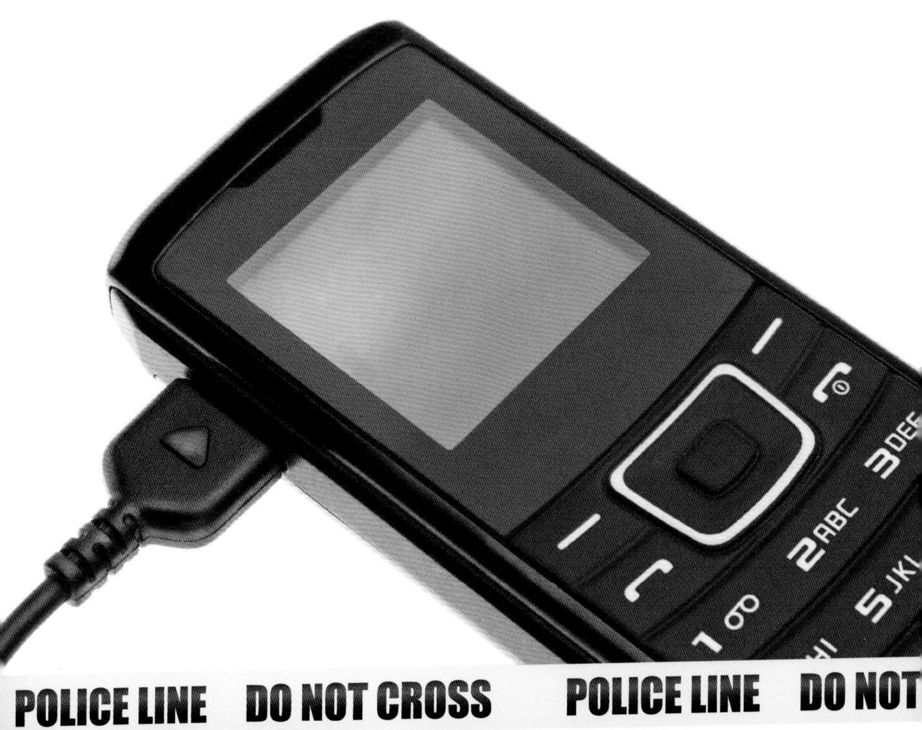
POLICE LINE DO NOT CROSS POLICE LINE
POLICE LINE DO NOT CROSS POLICE LINE DO NOT
DO NOT CROSS POLICE LINE DO NOT CROSS

DUMBNUTS WAS HERE

Two teenage vandals, let's call them John Smith and Mike Jones, set about a children's activity centre with relish. Having set off fire extinguishers, smashed plates and cups, and generally made a total war zone of the building, they felt sufficiently calmed to take out their colouring pens and draw graffiti all over the walls. Standard practice for this kind of incident, you might think. Well, yes, except you have to be remarkably stupid to write 'John Smith was here' at the scene of the crime, if that's your name. Which is what John Smith did.

The inspector in charge said: 'This crime is up there with the dumbest of all in the criminal league.'

COMPOUNDING THE (CRAP) CRIME

A 31-year-old man was pulled over by police for driving a stolen vehicle. The officers, who had heard pretty much every excuse for theft possible to imagine, were nevertheless dumbfounded when the driver explained that he had broken into the car in order to get to the local police station . . . to turn himself in for another crime. They were only surprised he hadn't stopped to commit a robbery en route.

MITIGATION PLEA At least he had a driving licence.

NICE NEIGHBOURHOOD

Police in New Jersey were at the scene of a stabbing, talking to a woman who had witnessed the incident. She was pointing out where the assault had happened, and in which direction the assailant had run off. Imagine their surprise when 35-year-old Emilio Johnson sauntered up behind them, slipped into the woman's car, which still had the key in the ignition, and drove off. He was arrested soon after and easily identified by the officers, who couldn't quite believe anyone would be that stupid.

VERDICT Sometimes a hire car is all you need.

DO NOT CROSS

'I'M SORRY, YOUR ACCOUNT APPLICATION HAS BEEN REJECTED'

Some robbers try to blend in to their surroundings a little too much before they commit a crime. Consider one would-be bank robber who walked into her target bank, decided there were too many customers waiting and thought it better to allow some of them to leave before proceeding with the stick-up. Anxious not to attract attention, she took an account application and filled it in – with a degree of honesty unworthy of such an accomplished criminal: name, address, telephone number and photo ID were all 100 per cent accurate. Once the bank was less crowded, the criminal mastermind advanced to the cashier, handed over the application form, pulled out her gun and demanded the cash in the teller's till. She escaped the bank without a hitch but regrettably left behind her contact details. The police tracked her down in less time than it takes to say 'Application failed'.

PERSONAL IN

NAME (LAST NAME FIRST

RESENT ADDRESS

MANEN

NO PAIN, NO GAIN

Rosie Ruiz astonished the marathon world in 1980 with her performance in the Boston Marathon. Finishing the race in, at that time, a record-breaking 2:31:56, she earned the immediate respect of her fellow competitors and the athletics world in general. Sadly that respect didn't last. Her dash out of the crowd half a mile from the finish line had been spotted by some of the spectators and her lack of tiredness ('I woke up with a lot of energy this morning'), perspiration and, in fact, general fitness provoked suspicion and then disqualification.

ANGER MANAGEMENT

27-year-old Jeremy Hunt from Kansas got into an argument with a woman at a bus stop. His temper rose to the point that he started to shout at her. Alarmed, the woman pulled her mobile out of her bag to call the police. Hunt reacted furiously and punched her full in the face. An elderly good Samaritan intervened but the younger man hit him with a blue folder and made off, dropping the folder as he ran away.

The police were called and managed to track the young man down in record time. How? The blue folder contained papers which included his name and his anger management homework.

Let's assume he had only just started attending the classes.

SENTENCE Ten years in solitary.

DIRTY TRICKS . . .

Three people working for a septic tank company in Florida tricked customers out of over $1 million by saying that they needed special toilet paper to avoid ruining their septic tanks. The crap scammers tricked a dozen victims so convincingly that some bought enough paper to last over 70 years.

SENTENCE Five years and full-time slopping out duties.

SOME DISGUISES WORK BETTER THAN OTHERS . . .

As a Scarborough man found when he held up a shop while wearing a motorcycle helmet to disguise his features from the CCTV. Unfortunately he'd forgotten that his name was emblazoned on the front of the helmet, and therefore his part in the robbery was filmed with a full credit in the titles.

SENTENCE Warning – check in the mirror before manoeuvring.

IT SEEMED LIKE A GOOD IDEA AT THE TIME . . .

Jeffrey Pick of Carson City, Michigan, felt that his complaints about being harassed by someone were being ignored. To attract proper police attention, he convinced a friend to shoot him in the shoulder with a shotgun and claimed the shot was fired by the harasser. The police took a different view, however: he was convicted of filing a false police report and now faces up to four years in jail and lengthy rehabilitation for his shoulder.

CAME OUT IN THE WASH

A man had been asked by his sister to move her washing machine to their mother's house but, being a bit strapped for cash, the budding entrepreneur cannily sold the £400 device for £150, no questions asked. When it came to explaining away the lost washing machine, though, he was somewhat less ingenious. He described in detail to his sister how the machine had fallen off the roof of his car while he was driving over a speed bump trying to escape from the, um, police on an unrelated matter. Not even blood proved thicker than this excuse, and his sister shopped him.

'If certificates were being given out for the brains of Britain, I think he would be the last individual to get one,' said his lawyer.

SENTENCE Laundry duty.

NINE, NINE, NEIN

When a German woman's house was burgled, two police officers called round to assess the break-in and take evidence. The victim was so taken with one of the officers that she called emergency services asking that the handsome bobby return to take down, um, further details. The police officer returned to find the burgled woman offering tea, sympathy and her phone number but no further details relevant to the crime. Her advances repelled, her shame was compounded by the target of her lust presenting her with a charge of wasting police time.

TWITS TWO

When the first Harry Potter film came out, the general public suddenly discovered that what was missing in their lives was their very own Hedwig. Owls, however, are relatively rare stock items in pet shops and so the inevitable black market sprang up. In Lancashire, two teenagers on the lookout to turn a quick profit identified a family who owned Suzie, a beautiful mature barn owl. They broke in one night and grabbed Suzie, stole a neighbour's car to make their escape and sped off.

Things started to go wrong when the neighbour spotted them and reported the car theft to the police, who gave chase. Meanwhile, inside the car, the owlnappers faced an unexpected problem – owls have both a huge wing span (up to a metre) and very sharp claws, and Suzie was upset at being snatched. It quickly became a case of felons versus talons. Talons won. The teenagers, with the police on their tail and an irate owl in the stolen vehicle, decided to reduce the number of problems they faced. Unnoticed at the time by the police, they pushed Suzie out of the car and continued their high-speed escape – bleeding profusely.

Eventually, like all car chases you see on *Police, Camera, Action!* the young, dumb crims abandoned the stolen car and attempted to flee on foot. They didn't get very far. It was only when police reviewed the CCTV footage to see if they had committed any further crimes in making their escape that they were able to identify Suzie as the object that had been ejected from the car. The boys faced prosecution for car and owl jacking.

'HELLO, IT'S ME AGAIN . . .'

A 45-year-old unemployed man, Neil Skeets, was charged with abusing the emergency line in 2008. The unusual charge came after it emerged that this lonely man had made over 27,000 calls to 911 'because they were free'. It seems that Skeets had no one in his life and would often call hundreds of times per day just for company. The police tracked him down after they traced his number. He apologised many, many times over but still faced a fine of up to six months in jail – where at least he would have some company.

POLICE LINE DO NOT CROSS POLICE LINE DO NOT
POLICE LINE DO NOT CROSS POLICE LINE DO NOT
DO NOT CROSS POLICE LINE DO NOT CROSS

NINE DOUBLE ONE

Foodie Letitia Osbourne gave the police both barrels in Atlanta when she reported a meal crime. She was outraged when presented with a McDouble instead of what she had ordered – Chicken McNuggets. The restaurant had apparently run out of the chicken delicacy and this drove Osbourne to call 911. 'This is an emergency. If I had known they didn't have McNuggets, I wouldn't have given my money, and now she wants to give me a McDouble, but I don't want one.' The police disagreed with her and charged her with abusing the 911 service.

PULL THE OTHER ONE

Crap calls to emergency services aren't confined to the West. In China there is an increasing tendency to panic and ring 110 (the equivalent of 911 or 999) when faced with the slightest problem. One recent domestic incident serves to highlight the issue. Officer Seng was dispatched to an apartment in Dingbo after the operator received two calls from the same couple in short succession. The first was from a woman who complained that her boyfriend had refused to rub her feet; the second from the boyfriend, furious that his girlfriend was being so demanding. Not exactly the kind of 'domestic' you see on *CSI*. The officer talked the couple through their emergency dispute and both parties ended up happy. Domestic bliss restored, the officer cautioned them for wasting police time.

110
2
ABC
5

UP IN SMOKE

Spontaneous crime rarely pays, as our next example shows. In an extraordinary adventure, 'Clive' (we'll save his blushes) was inconvenienced by pub closing time and decided that he wanted to carry on drinking. As it happened he was passing a corner shop which he knew stocked lager, and lots of it. Without a second thought, as if a highly trained acrobat, Clive shinned up the drainpipe and leapt, feet first, down the chimney. The descent went well until about two-thirds of the way, when our agile offender got stuck in the flue. Really stuck.

This was when the perilousness of the situation stuck Clive – breathing in decades' worth of soot, stuck fast in the middle of a chimney in the dead of night, and with no way out . . .

At about five in the morning he started to shout for help. He was lucky that the shopkeeper, who always arrived early to sort the newspapers, heard the muffled shouts. He checked the shop, finding nothing amiss, but the noise didn't go away.

He called emergency services and within a short space of time they arrived to track down the source of the noise. Clive was located after his trainers were spotted lying in the grate of the fireplace. The fire brigade started to dismantle the chimney, brick by brick. After an hour, a pair of

naked feet were uncovered, followed by bare legs, and eventually Clive was freed from his suffocating prison. He was also completely naked. In trying to wiggle up and down, his tracksuit bottoms had slipped off and similarly his t-shirt had come off as he descended the chimney.

Now Clive had to explain exactly how he had come to be stuck in a chimney in the middle of the night. In true crap-criminal fashion he came up with a crap excuse: he'd been trying to avoid drug dealers who were after him. Now not only could he be done for breaking and entering, he was likely to get involved in a drugs charge as well.

CRAP BANKING

Many people think what bankers get away with is criminal but, even by today's credit-crunching standards, what trader Nick Leeson didn't quite get away with was staggering. He caused the collapse of Barings, the UK's oldest merchant bank (which counted HM the Queen among its glittering customers), thereby rendering 1,200 people unemployed.

Leeson was Barings Bank's chief trader in the Singapore stock exchange in the early 1990s and, fatally, he was given the scope to do pretty much as he pleased – unchecked. Initially he did very well, earning over three times his annual salary in bonuses, and generating about ten per cent of the bank's profits in one year. He lived the champagne lifestyle with his wife Lisa, and everyone was happy.

Sadly for him, and the bank, this state of affairs didn't last long, and he started making losses. On one occasion he bet the markets would stay pretty stable overnight, only to see them rocked by the economic fallout from the Kobe earthquake in Japan. To cover his accumulating losses, he hid them in an account numbered '88888' – '8' being a Chinese symbol for good luck. But his luck had well and truly run out by now and, like a gambler at the bookies, he kept making bigger and bigger bets on the markets in an attempt to recoup his disastrous losses.

Not surprisingly this approach failed, and as his losses reached a gobsmacking £827 million ($1.3 billion), which was more than the total capital and reserves of the bank, Leeson fled with his wife to Malaysia, leaving a note saying, 'I'm sorry.' Sadly for him, this didn't really cover it, and the bank was declared insolvent a month later, in February 1995. Leeson served four years in a Singapore prison for his crime before returning to Britain, where he now gives lectures on risk management. You really couldn't make it up.

DUH ENRON-RON-RON, DUH ENRON-RON

Enron went from being a middling energy company to America's seventh-largest corporation by the end of the 1990s. How did it achieve this? The usual mix of insider dealing, offshore accounting and cooking the books.

Deregulation of the energy market helped – allowing the company to sell natural gas at much higher prices than had previously been allowed. The profits Enron gained from this were used to accumulate a vast range of assets – and liabilities. The problem was, they exaggerated the assets and played down the liabilities, encouraging investment by erroneous and misleading accountancy.

When people became suspicious, noting the drive-a-bus-through-it discrepancy between the company's high stock value and its earnings, Enron's CEO Jeffrey Skilling acted aggressively, calling one journalist 'unethical' (for failing to properly research the state of the company) and responding to criticism from a respected Wall Street analyst with: 'Thank you very much. We appreciate that . . . asshole.' This played well with besotted colleagues, but outside of the organisation it looked like a sign of desperation – which it was.

Further investigation of Enron's financial statements revealed a lot more natural gas than solid assets and it eventually filed for bankruptcy in 2001 with staggering losses – the company owed creditors $67 billion. Thousands of people lost their jobs. To top it all off, many of the corporation's contributions to its employees' pension pots had been made in the form of company shares (perfectly normal practice in America) so retiring workers were massively out of pocket too. Skilling and other executive officers were sentenced to lengthy spells inside, raising the question: who's the asshole now?

SNOW JOKE

It's a mystery that wouldn't even tax Scooby-Doo (let alone Thelma). A father and son 'team' were charged with burglary after they broke into a dairy in New Zealand and stole ice cream and frozen chips. So far, so ordinary. What marks this example of petty theft out from many others is that the break-in happened in the middle of winter, after a huge dump of snow. The family felons escaped the scene with their bizarre bounty and walked the 2km home – leaving a clean set of footprints in their wake. The police officer in charge commented: 'We're not typically amused by burglary but one must look at the stupidity of it, especially given what they actually stole.'

Apparently no stimulating or intoxicating substances influenced the crime.

STILL UNLIKELY TO OFFEND

- It is legal for a citizen of Chester to shoot a Welshman with a bow and arrow if he remains in the city after sunset.
- It is illegal for a Welshman to enter the city of Chester before sunrise.
- It is legal for a man to beat his wife once a month in Arkansas – but not more than once.
- It is illegal to own a feather bed in Buenos Aires.
- It is legal to have sexual relations with animals in twelve countries throughout the world and fourteen states in the US.

METAL BRA

This is a clear example of not thinking through your crime. A woman attempted to smuggle about 50g of cannabis out of New Zealand by wrapping the drug up in little packets made of tin foil. Good thinking – the foil stops the sniffer dogs picking up the scent. Unfortunately it also sets off the metal detectors at airports and, even if you hide the packets in your underwear, you're still going to get searched.

KIDS ON THE HOOD

Child travel has been known to test the sanity of even the most level-headed parent. The usual solution is to buy a car the size of a minibus, so the little darlings can be kept as far away from mummy and daddy as possible.

Washington couple Ryan Jennings and Jane Smith decided to take things a step further and, in a move which may well fail to catch on in wider society, strapped their four offspring – aged between four and eight – to the hood of their saloon car and then proceeded to drive to a neighbourhood liquor store.

The manager of the store witnessed Jennings checking the strap across the hood was tight enough – child safety obviously being of paramount concern – before getting back in the car and setting off. The store manager called the police, who stopped the car shortly afterwards. A belligerent, reeking-of-booze Jennings slurred: 'It was only a short journey – I thought they'd like it.' The police disagreed and charged him with child neglect and drink driving.

CRIMEBOOK

'It makes our job a lot easier when basically they post what amounts to a confession on the internet for everyone to see,' said Sergeant Gould, after police in Montreal had apprehended three out of four teenagers involved in a robbery.

The teenage gang had robbed a supermarket in the city with consummate professionalism. They escaped clutching about $10,000, plus a pile of cigarettes and sweets. But their professionalism in committing the crime was not matched by their ability to cover their tracks. Instead of enjoying the bounty in private, the teenagers did as teenagers do and posted a video on, er, Facebook, in which they bragged about their haul. A concerned family member tipped the police off.

STATUS UPDATE Busted.

THE MYSTERY OF THE BULGARIAN DRIVER

Speeding tickets land on everyone's doormat eventually. One family in Kent, though, found one morning that two had arrived. It seems that both parents had committed separate offences on the same day. The combined fines and penalty points drove them to consider extreme evasive action. They hatched a plan to claim that someone else had been driving one of their cars. The fictional culprit was based on a Bulgarian taxi driver they had met on holiday in Sofia the previous year – let's call him Mr K. The couple wrote to explain their innocence on one count of speeding. However their explanation was so contrived that the adjudicator smelled a speeding rat and passed the claim on to the police, who asked for further proof.

With hindsight, the couple acknowledges that this was the time to put an end to their scheme and pay up. But no, instead they rose to the challenge. They decided to provide a statement from Mr K, sent from Bulgaria. How? Simple – the wife booked a flight to Sofia and, on arrival, found a handy souvenir shop selling postcards and stamps. Safely holed up in her hotel she wrote an affectionate and grateful postcard to herself from Mr K, hoping that his stay hadn't inconvenienced them and that he'd very much enjoyed the use of their car.

Genius. Or not. When the couple handed the postcard over to the police, suspicions mounted to the point that the officer in charge contacted Interpol to try to track down Mr K. Oh dear. Our speeding couple had now managed to instigate a Europe-wide manhunt.

When Interpol turned up no evidence that Mr K existed, the police charged the couple with perverting the course of justice. At last, husband and wife realised the game was up and pleaded guilty. They were fined £9,200 and ordered to pay court costs of £1,900. The initial fines of £120 had cost them nearly £12,000 in fines, flights and fees. Doh!

OLDSMOBILE

Many parents rely heavily on their own parents for additional childcare these days. A Texan couple, however, had second thoughts after the grandparents of their 7-year-old daughter were arrested for getting drunk and towing her behind their SUV in a plastic toy car. The car was secured by a couple of dog leads. The child, wearing only a swimsuit and no protective clothing or headwear, was thankfully not injured by the experience.

58-year-old grandfather Hank Bender, who was driving the SUV, turned his bloodshot eyes on the arresting police officer and informed him that he could not produce his licence as it had been revoked ten years previously – for driving under the influence, naturally.

During the drive, Bender's wife Lianne, also drunk, was sitting in the back of the vehicle with the door open, happily encouraging her granddaughter during her premature driving lesson. She later told police that they were just having fun and had been doing it all day. Her son, summoned to take back his daughter, simply asked his mum, 'are you f**king stupid?' Bender was charged with child cruelty, drink driving and driving with a revoked licence.

Next Christmas in the Bender household should be interesting!

VERDICT Don't let your parents drive you (or your child) round the bend.

LICE LINE DO NOT CROSS POLICE LINE DO NOT CR

POLICE LINE DO NOT CROSS POLICE LINE DO NO

POLICE LINE DO NOT CROSS POLICE LINE DO NOT

NE DO NOT CROSS POLICE LINE DO NOT CROSS

SORRY BILL

A man walks into a busy petrol station in Arkansas and buys some cigarettes with a $100 bill. He walks out but returns, having forgotten to buy matches. Unfortunately there he meets a police officer examining the cash he just handed over. This is where the crap crime comes in. The note lacked the smack of authenticity that most might expect of even a fairly feeble attempted forgery. The first problem was that when the cashier looked again at the note, after he had served the other customers in the shop, he discovered that the ink was still slightly wet. The other problem was that the picture of the president lacked a face and, on closer examination, had the legend 'Clinton' underneath it.

Despite our sophisticated forger's claims that he thought the, ah, 'bill' was genuine, he was arrested and charged with counterfeiting money.

The police officer commented: 'Of all the cases I've worked with phoney money, this is the sorriest bill I've ever seen.'

100

CRAPPING CRIME

A 22-year-old resident of Ohio, Leon Harris, was recovering in a local hospital after police took him there from his jail cell. He was treated for injuries to his rectum, which 'may have occurred' as a result of his attempt to conceal a 10-inch .38 barrel revolver internally. Harris – who was arrested for speeding, resisting arrest and being found in possession of marijuana – was strip searched before being confined to the cell. He claimed he had found the gun in the cell toilet, and that 'someone was trying to kill him'. The gun was unloaded.

VERDICT Concealing a weapon can be a pain in the arse.

STOOL PIGEON

It's probably not in *Guinness World Records* but if it was, 32-year-old George Deakin might just win the 'stuff up your butt' category.

Deakin was pulled over by police in Maryland late at night after they noticed his vehicle swerving erratically.

During a routine pat down, the traffic officer 'felt a hard object, like a plum' near to, but separate from, Deakin's genital area. Suspicious now, the police obtained a search warrant and took him to a nearby hospital, where an X-ray revealed a foreign object concealed in his rectum. A dose of laxatives later, Deakin passed over 80 crack rocks from his bottom, wrapped in plastic bags. Quite a haul. He wasn't done.

When a subsequent X-ray showed further hidden bounty, Deakin was returned to the throne, where he expelled two bags containing over 200 tablets of a powerful painkiller.

Still not done, and presumably running out of copies of *Ideal Home* to read, Deakin managed to drop a final log of 12 grams of marijuana, before being taken to a cell for a well-deserved lie down, and several charges of possession.

VERDICT When you've got to go . . .

POLICE LINE
DO NOT CROSS
POLICE LINE
DO NOT
POLICE LINE
DO NOT CROSS
POLICE LINE
DO NOT

TWIT TWEETS

A dumb London looter's dawning realisation that bragging about your crime on Twitter may not be all that clever – ennit!

'Got tones [sic] of stuff today!!!!!!!!! #whop whop'	14 hours ago
'@------------- I ain't gonna get caught u fag'	1 hour ago
'@------------- wat ev;; it was free so I took it ennit,, didn't get caught so' 1 hour ago	1 hour ago
'its not like I can tke da stuff back nw ppl;; I realize wat I did ws rong [sic] nw'	2 minutes ago

STATUS UPDATE #fail – wat evs!

LICE LINE DO NOT CROSS POLICE LINE DO NOT CR

POLICE LINE DO NOT CROSS POLICE LINE DO NOT

POLICE LINE DO NOT CROSS POLICE LINE DO NOT

NE DO NOT CROSS POLICE LINE DO NOT CROSS

AMISHED THE SIGN OFFICER!

Ohio police ended up in not-so-high-speed pursuit of an Amish teenager driving a horse and carriage. The 16-year-old boy, who was in illegal possession of alcohol, failed to halt at a stop sign. This instigated a mile-long pursuit in third gear by nearby traffic officers. The, er, 'chase' ended when the boy abandoned the vehicle in a ditch and fled on foot, only to be arrested by the somewhat speedier cops, who charged him with reckless driving, failure to yield to an emergency vehicle and underage possession of alcohol.

VERDICT When trying to escape from the police, think horses for courses.

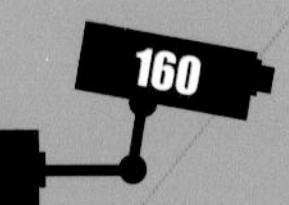

NEXT
2 MILES

JUST A LITTLE PRICK

A South African would-be assassin had a lucky escape when he pricked himself with the tip of a poison-filled umbrella spike while demonstrating the Bond villain-style equipment to his accomplice.

Fortunately for him, he failed to inject himself with enough of the deadly liquid and made a full recovery. However his run of luck didn't continue – the hapless duo discovered one of their assassination targets had moved abroad, and the other target couldn't be found in spite of their, ahem, 'best' attempts to trace him. They gave up and threw the umbrella in a nearby river, no doubt just as it started raining.

GETTING THE NUMBERS WRONG

A motorist was arrested after police clocked him driving at 104mph in a 60mph zone. The arresting officer had been tipped off by a concerned fellow motorist who said that the driver had been shouting into his phone, waving a cigarette around and changing lanes erratically. When questioned, the man claimed that due to his dyslexia, he thought he was travelling at an entirely safe 041mph. This defence crumbled when it was pointed out that his speedometer was a needle-and-dial design.

TOO FAST!

EMAIL SCAM – SO CRAP YOU'D NEVER FALL FOR IT . . .

ATTN: SIR/MADAM [*nice personal touch*]

First I must solicit your confidence in this transaction, this is by virtue of its nature top secret [*so 'top secret' that you are sending it to three million people*]. Though I know that a transaction of this magnitude will make any one apprehensive [*well, you would think*], but I am assuring you that all will be well at the end of the day [*oh good*].

I am MR Moses Joseph the manager with the ----- Bank of Nigeria Plc, Lagos . . . An American Brad Johnson (Snr.) an oil engineer with the Federal Government until his death in a tragic automobile accident [*unfortunate assassination / careless gardening episode*] banked with us, and had a closing balance worth US$10,000,000. Valuable efforts are being made to get in touch with any of the Johnson's family but

to no success [*you'd think it not beyond the realms of possibility that they have received this email*]. The Board of Directors has arranged for the fund to be declared 'Unclaimed'. In order to avert this negative development I now seek your permission to have you stand as next of kin to Late Brad Johnson (Snr.) so that the fund US$10 Million will be paid into your account as the beneficiary's next of kin [*wait a minute – this sounds almost too good to be true!*] I am assuring you that this business is 100% Risk Free involvement [*well that's OK then*]. If this proposal is acceptable by you, please reply furnishing me with your Bank Name, Bank Account Number, and Address [*OK – but you'll probably need a password so that's included too*]. The sharing of the fund are thus: 30% for you the account owner, 60% for I and the remaining 10% for expenses for both parties. Please not make undue advantage of the trust I have bestowed in you [*wouldn't dream of it*]. Best regards, MR Moses Joseph.

... OR WOULD YOU?

A county treasurer from the United States was sentenced to ten years in jail for embezzling over $1 million in county funds in an email scam case. Ted Bunson, Treasurer of ---- County, was sending the money through his own accounts to the perpetrators, in spite of warnings from friends and colleagues that he was being scammed. Bunson had even notified his local bank to expect a payment of millions of dollars into a reactivated old account. Strangely, the money never arrived!

And the son of a prominent US neuroscientist filed a lawsuit claiming his father had squandered $1.5 million of his family's fortune, over a ten-year period, in payments to Nigerian criminals, in expectation of a similarly large sum. The doctor had even travelled to Nigeria, it was claimed, to meet with a shadowy figure called 'The General' – in order to convince the scammers that he was genuine!

According to experts, one way to convince yourself that the scam is for real is to send more money – energy bills seem to work the same way . . .

THIS NOTE IS LEGAL TENDER FOR ALL DEBTS, PUBLIC AND PRIVATE

DOING TIME DURING A CRIME

We've all experienced the sensation that life is passing us by as we queue to buy stamps, pay a bill or buy some dog food. So a twinge of empathy for the bank robber who left the scene of his own crime, because the wait was getting him down, wouldn't be unnatural.

The man entered a Nashville bank shortly before closing time, and slipped a note across the counter demanding all the money in the bank and informing the teller that, yes, he did have a gun in his pocket.

The teller started to collect money from his till while the would-be robber twiddled his thumbs, smiled politely at other waiting customers and, not surprisingly, kept glancing at his watch.

After a few minutes he sighed, complained that the teller was taking too long, and turned and left the premises empty-handed, shaking his head.

Detective Randy Mayer, from the Nashville police, smirked as he later suggested to reporters that the man should maybe just have asked for 'SOME of the money'.

VERDICT Bank queues can be criminal.

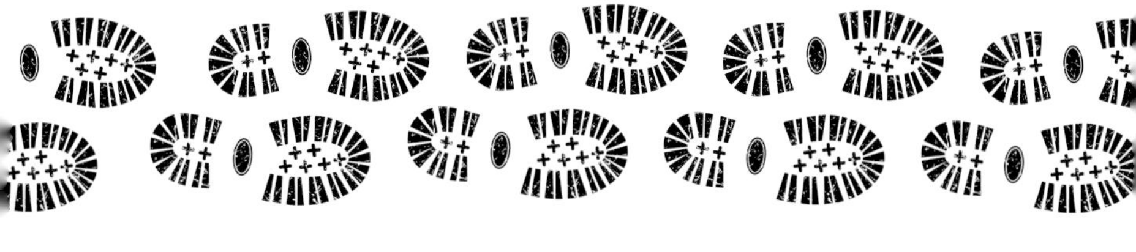

THINKING OUTSIDE THE BOX

It was a truly ingenious crime. The judge later called it 'unique, cunning and daring'. Sadly, it also failed.

Manuel Lopez hid himself inside the cargo hold of a plane bound for London which he knew contained over 1.5 million euros. He had already arranged for two boxes addressed to a safe place to be loaded onto the plane. The plan was simple: he would steal the euros from their container, put the money into one of the boxes and himself into the other. When the plane landed, he and his loot would be dispatched to the safe house while the container that had contained the money would be delivered empty.

Lopez managed to sneak into the cargo hold, find the boxes addressed to the safe house and locate the euro stash. However the bulk of the money was in a container that he wouldn't be able to reseal after he had cracked it open. There was one smaller haul he could steal without rousing suspicion, which he duly did – deciding to carry it with him in the box he'd allocated for himself rather than use the other. Lopez sat inside the box with his stash and waited to be unloaded and delivered.

The plan worked until that random event occurred that can scupper any genius idea. Baggage handlers arrived to remove the cargo. In the process of moving the boxes they dropped the one in which our mastermind was squatting. It split open on impact with the tarmac – revealing Lopez and his loot. According to one of the handlers, he casually said, 'don't worry about me, I'm all right,' before walking off leaving the loot behind. He might even have gotten away with it if he hadn't cut his thumb on the crate, leaving a juicy DNA sample for the police to match once the crime had come to light.

CASE CLOSED

Barcelona airport had been suffering a spate of thefts from the cargo area, and airport security were on alert to look out for anything suspicious, so when a member of staff saw a man struggling to lift a suitcase on to an airport bus, he alerted the police.

At first sight of their uniforms, the traveller sped off. The police cautiously approached the suitcase. Noticing that it looked wet and smelled, the men in uniform concluded that it probably wasn't explosive and gave it a hefty kick before unzipping it to reveal a large Polish man. His excuse – 'I couldn't afford the fare' – wasn't that convincing and it was undermined by the fact that he was wearing a head torch, had a tool for opening zips and locks, and carried a stash of stolen loot.

Definitely an open and shut case . . .

TOY STORIES

The subject of this story is an extraordinary criminal who nearly didn't make it into these pages. A man with over 40 successful robberies under his belt who was also charming, careful and efficient. Of course it couldn't last. He finally got caught while robbing a fast food restaurant and was given a custodial sentence. Undeterred, he made a dramatic escape by sneaking under a delivery truck and holding on to the chassis as it drove off. No, this doesn't just happen in the movies . . .

Our competent hero took further steps to put distance between himself and the law by adopting a new identity in a small community. Claiming to have a 'secret' government job, he joined the local church and rapidly became a pillar of the community, warming the locals' hearts by distributing toys to children. He became, in the space of six months, a model citizen.

Unfortunately his daytime hours were not spent doing the government's dirty work but rather hiding out in the stockroom of the local Toys'R'Us. This may of course go some way to explain his generosity to the local children.

As Christmas approached and the store became busier the chances of being discovered in the hidey-hole grew. He spent his nights

burrowing into a vacant shop next door and installed himself in the basement. Things might have worked out if the ingenious crim hadn't found the temptation to return to his previous career irresistible.

One evening, armed with a toy pistol from a pawn shop he'd turned over, Toy Store Man came out of hiding and attempted to hold up his former sanctuary. Sadly for him the two toy shop assistants screamed and fled, deciding they weren't paid enough to go through a stick-up. With no chance of opening the safe, he abandoned his plan, his cubby hole and his life as a local do-gooder. The police soon found his hideout and managed to piece together his identity from the clues he left behind. The children of the town were devastated.

CRIME IS TIRING

Snoring can create problems for a lot of people – even the snorer. One man for whom this is true was a member of a three-man gang intent on stealing copper pipes from a Los Angeles restaurant. The not-very-heavy metal band had parked their removal truck in an alleyway behind the restaurant and were busy in the basement extracting the pipes, when some police officers in a patrol car noticed the vehicles and became suspicious.

The police made their move and grabbed two of the felons but spent the next two hours searching the neighbourhood for the third. Having found not a trace of him, they returned to the scene of the crime and began a systematic hunt of the restaurant. One officer heard what he thought was a drill and presumed that the gang, in their hasty attempted escape, had failed to turn the power tool off. Locating the source of the sound the policeman found our third metal-head asleep on top of a fridge, snoring loudly. Apparently he had dozed off while he was hiding.

HEAD IN THE iClouds

If you're going to steal a smartphone, it's probably not the brightest idea to use it to take photos of yourself that then upload to a file-sharing website, where the previous owner can view them with ease.

Yet that's what one man decided to do. When a tourist lost her phone during a Mediterranean cruise, she assumed that she must have left it at one of the stop-off points visited by the ship. Imagine her surprise, then, when photos of a young man in the uniform of the cruise company began appearing on the internet site linked to her camera phone.

When she sent one of the smiling portraits to the head office of the organisation, they confirmed that the photogenic young man had indeed been serving her drinks at sunset merely a month before. She got her phone back when the ship returned to port and the crew member was placed on 'administrative leave'. Somehow we feel his cruising days may be over.

VERDICT Mugshots should only be taken by the police.

MINOR INFRINGEMENT

Inappropriate romantic entanglements happen at all stages of life. Sometimes they can just prove awkward; other times they are bad for your family, career and your life in general. Such was the case for Anne-Marie Sheldon, a Latin teacher in Michigan. Her daughter was going out with a classmate – both of them underage – when boyfriend and mother started casting glances at each other. Anne-Marie, 46, decided to move things on a stage by sending a provocative self-portrait to his mobile phone. Failing to get a reaction she sent an even more provocative one, at which point the boy's father happened to pick up the phone and discover all.

A little short of cash at the time, he sent a blackmail note demanding, well, an Xbox in return for his eternal silence (it appears that the going rate for topless pictures these days is measured in consoles not cash). She refused, so the father demanded she sell her wedding ring and give him the cash. Again she refused, but this time she was smart enough to involve the police by reporting the father for extortion. The slight problem when she explained the situation to the attentive officers was how to explain the presence of the pictures on the minor's phone.

The police were even-handed in dealing with the crime: she was charged with disseminating matter harmful to juveniles and the father with extortion. There is no information as to whether their son and daughter are still romantically involved.

SENTENCE Write out 100 times: '*ego picturas dissolutas ad pupillos non mittam* (I will not send provocative pictures to minors)'

WITCH TRIAL

'Eye of toad and tongue of newt, please convert this spell to LOOT'

It seems that there is still a lot of belief in the power of witchcraft in Romania, and two entrepreneurial women tried to use this to their advantage. They reinvented themselves as witches (let's call them Griselda and Wanda) and targeted prominent public figures, demanding cash in return for casting protective or life-enhancing spells – shielding one victim from his mother-in-law, for example.

Griselda and Wanda went to some lengths to convince their victims of the veracity of their potions and charms – they performed Hammer House of Horror-style animal sacrifices in graveyards in, yep, the dead of night. They then branched out into elaborate Voodoo rituals to increase the impact of their work. The problem was that the spells didn't actually work. Surprisingly. They started to get complaints, and disgruntled clients tried to tear up their agreements. When threatened, the witches turned up the heat, saying they would start to cast spells on the victims and would reveal their embarrassing personal secrets (like the fact they had employed witches). All to no avail; they were arrested and later bailed pending trial on counts of extortion.

HI! KARATE?

'Do your homework' is a saying one Colombian burglar must wish he'd taken more notice of before setting out one fine day for a spot of breaking and entering in the city of Manizales.

Having negotiated the security precautions of his chosen property, and helped himself to a laptop, some cameras and other sundry goods, he was rudely interrupted by the pan-American karate champion – well it was his home, after all! To make matters worse for the hapless thief, the champion's pals, also karate experts, were there to extend a warm welcome and, er, 'apprehend' him. The arrival of the police was for once welcomed by the wrongdoer, who probably should have stayed in bed, or tried to rob a bank instead.

VERDICT Should have checked out the trophy cabinet before loading up the swag bag . . .

RIEN N'EST DANS LA MANIÈRE DE DÉJEUNER!

Useless French bank robber Alain Dupont could put his failed heist down to bad timing. Having driven to the bank's car park at 12.45 pm, and spent fifteen minutes in his car, no doubt psyching himself up for his moment of glory, Dupont impressively burst from the vehicle, ski mask on, shotgun in hand, and rushed to the bank's entrance only to find it had closed for lunch at 1 pm on the dot. '*Merde*!' he must have thought to himself.

Unfortunately for him the bank's security guard was still on the premises and saw every moment of this spectacular attempt, as well as noting Dupont's licence number, which the police used to track him down shortly afterwards. Oh well, *c'est la vie*!

VERDICT *Si la banque est fermée, vous ne pouvez pas voler d'elle* :(

LICE LINE DO NOT CROSS POLICE LINE DO NOT CR

POLICE LINE DO NOT CROSS POLICE LINE DO NOT

FERMÉ

POLICE LINE DO NOT CROSS POLICE LINE DO NOT

INE DO NOT CROSS POLICE LINE DO NOT CROSS

MY CREDIT'S NO GOOD HERE SIR!

A 40-year-old New Yorker was busted when he attempted to pay for a beer with a credit card belonging to the bartender!

According to police, Hank Jackson had broken into a car and made off with a wallet and some other personal items. Flushed with success, he decided to celebrate with a quiet drink at a nearby bar. Imagine the bartender's surprise when he was handed his own credit card to pay for the beer. Surprise soon turned to anger and he called the police, who arrested Jackson and charged him with theft and fraud.

VERDICT Always pay with cash if you're hopeless with cards.

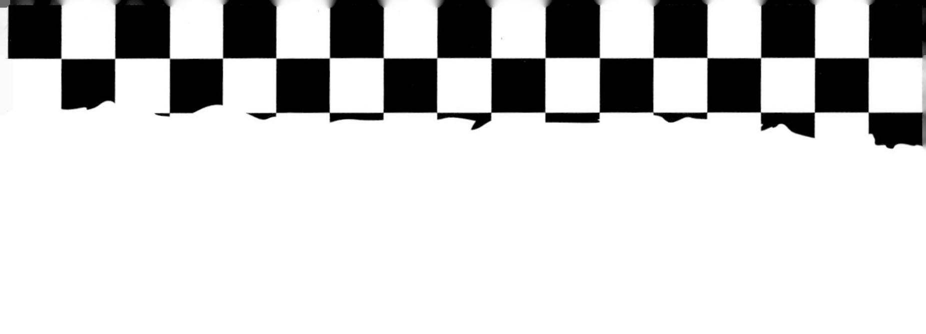

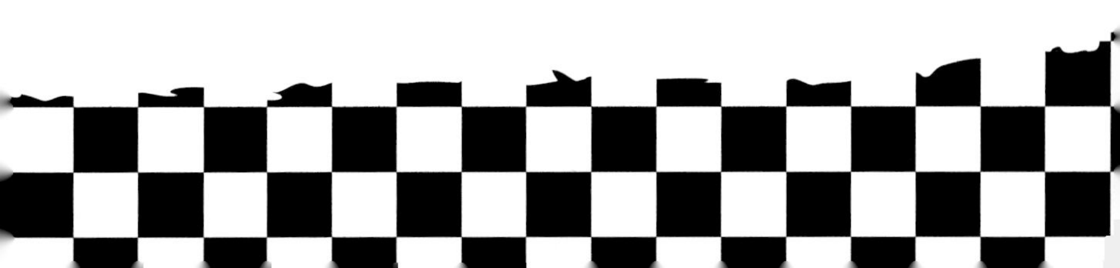

iCOLLISION

A pedestrian in Los Angeles sued not only the driver of the car that knocked her down on a highway but also Google, because she was using Google Maps for walking directions at the time.

ROAD SAFETY CODE UPDATE Look both ways and stop gawping at your smartphone when crossing a busy street.

COULD IT BE MAGIC?

A man took the magician David Copperfield to court, claiming that the magician was infringing his patent. The patent in question? His godly powers. Mr 'One Rabbit Short of a Trick' was convinced that the only explanation for Copperfield's tricks was supernatural power and therefore, logically, that constituted an infringement of his patent. Aside from the issue of proof, the litigation faltered on the fact that, mercifully, the patent was still pending. Case dismissed.

LICE LINE DO NOT CROSS POLICE LINE DO NOT CR

INE DO NOT CROSS POLICE LINE DO NOT CROSS

ON SHAKY GROUNDS

A stressed executive in California grabbed a takeout burger meal from a fast food chain on the way to a meeting. Driving along, he put the strawberry shake between his legs while he rummaged in the brown bag for the burger. He had to lean a bit further over than he was expecting, squeezed his thighs together and made the freezing shake burst all over his trousers. The shock caused him to drive into another car. He sued the fast food company but, like the shake, this proved fruitless and he was done for driving without due care and attention.

POLICE LINE
DO NOT CROSS
POLICE LINE
DO NOT CROSS
DO NOT CROSS
POLICE LINE
CROSS

SO HELP ME GOD

Having been convicted of grand larceny and breaking and entering, an inventive litigant sued himself for $5 million for violating his own civil rights and religious beliefs because he had allowed himself to get drunk and commit the crimes. He wrote:

'I partook of alcoholic beverages in 1993, July 1st, as a result I caused myself to violate my religious beliefs. This was done by my going out and getting arrested. I want to pay myself 5 million dollars but ask the state to pay it on my behalf since I can't work and am a ward of the state.' Ingenious it may have been, but the case was thrown out on the technical grounds of being 'totally ludicrous'.

SMILE YOU'RE ON (YOUR OWN) CANDID CAMERA!

A couple returned to their home in Nottingham and found it had been burgled: thousands of pounds-worth of jewellery, computer equipment, cameras and other gadgets stolen. The police were called but could find no leads. The next day a car was stopped in the city centre and a large quantity of the jewellery was discovered in the footwell of the passenger seat. The police, however, could not pin the burglary on the driver until they visited his home, where they found all the evidence they needed. The security-conscious burglar had his own CCTV system. In the footage retrieved by the police, four men (including the driver) were seen arriving at the house, getting out of the car wearing latex gloves and unloading the swag from the robbery.

VERDICT To preserve your freedom, remember to switch off all home appliances.

CCTV
in operation

NAMED DRIVER

Police in Baden-Baden, Germany, stopped a driver because his car had an illegal registration plate. Not wanting a conviction, the unfortunate dupe gave a false name. In a million-to-one chance coincidence, the name he supplied was of someone wanted for causing death by dangerous driving. *Scheiße*!

DO NOT CROSS
POLICE LINE
POLICE LINE
DO NOT CROSS
POLICE LINE
D
D
POLICE LINE
DO NOT CROSS
DO NOT CROSS
POLICE LINE

EXTRA ANCHOVIES WITH THE CASH PLEASE

If only bank robbery were as easy as ordering a takeaway. A bank in Lincoln, Nebraska, received a call from a young man one Monday morning asking that a bag containing $100,000 in large bills – without dye packs – be reserved for him and that he'd be in later in the day to collect it. The staff at the bank were just a tiny bit suspicious and notified the police. Sure enough, half an hour later two men turned up, complete with guns and masks, only to be nabbed by the waiting cops.

MEAT HEAD

Probably one of the dumbest things you can do if you're nabbed for something is claim you are someone well-known or (in this case) a global superstar. A man dressed as a vampire and, shall we say, clearly having had one rhesus positive over the eight, hijacked a taxi driving through Wichita, Kansas. When he was apprehended by police he claimed he was the singer Meat Loaf. Sadly he wasn't a Dead Ringer and was arrested for drink driving and vehicle theft.

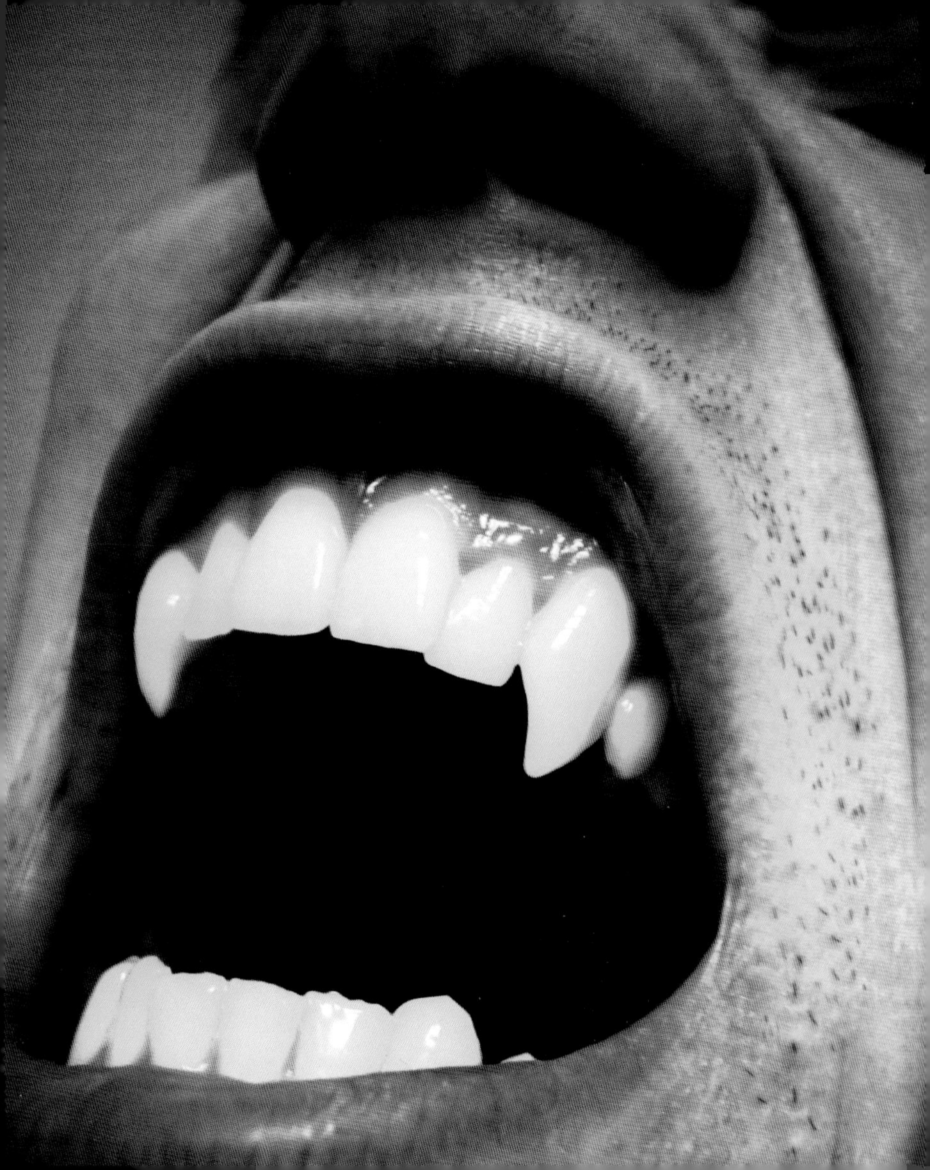

PRIVATES – KEEP OUT!

Holidaymakers at the Coconut Grove Spa Park in California were surprised when 22-year-old Wayne Swallow jumped the brick wall separating them from the outside world, but not as surprised as Swallow when he realised he had landed in a nudist resort.

He had been chased there by staff and customers of a nearby garden centre, who had witnessed him attempting a robbery. Swallow claimed later he had merely been shopping for mango and banana plants.

Once inside the naturist's holiday spa, Swallow pulled a knife and hijacked a golf buggy before attempting to flee. He was soon identified and arrested at the scene by police officers, who noticed he was the only person fully clothed. Conveniently for this story he had been on the run since April Fool's Day, some 50 days earlier.

VERDICT At a nudist resort, if you've got something to hide, stay outside!

BEYOND
THIS POINT
YOU MAY
ENCOUNTER
NUDE
SUNBATHERS

BUSTED BY LOTTERY TICKET

A 41-year-old woman from Rio de Janeiro claimed that she hadn't turned up to work one day because she had been kidnapped. The next day, a passer-by found Carmen Santos tied up on the backseat of her car, which was parked suspiciously close to her house. She said that she had been on her way to work the day before when an assailant had jumped into her car at some traffic lights, tied her up and then driven around doing drug deals. When the police searched her, they found a lottery ticket in her pocket that had been bought on the day of the alleged kidnap. Further investigation revealed CCTV footage of her withdrawing cash from an ATM at a petrol station before walking into the shop to buy the ticket – all while she was supposed to be suffering at the hands of the drug dealer. Carmen was charged with aggravated perjury. History does not record whether she won the lottery.

VERDICT Her numbers came up.

MEGA LOTTO
STATE PICK
YOUR CHANCE TO PICK THE WINNER
THIS WEEKS A DOUBLE ROLL OVER
A. 02 12 13 18 32 38
B. 01 02 10 11 25 42
C. 11 18 22 36 37 38
D. 12 22 25 28 36 39
E. 09 10 13 19 40 43
F. 05 06 19 20 28 32

PRESIDENT OF CRAP CRIMINALS

An Austrian man, unobtrusively disguised in a Barack Obama mask, attempted to rob a bank in downtown Vienna. When he tried to enter the building, though, he found the doors were locked. The bank had been closed early for staff training. He started to hammer on the doors with the fake pistol he had brought along with him, frustrated because the employees were clearly visible inside. In what turned out to be a very enjoyable spectator sport, the staff found that the more they laughed the more agitated the would-be robber became.

'We thought it was part of the training, some sort of initiative test, or a joke. Laughing only seemed to make him more angry,' said one employee.

The robber president eventually spotted the sign on the door and made his grumpy exit from the scene.

LICE LINE DO NOT CROSS POLICE LINE DO NOT CR

POLICE LINE DO NOT CROSS POLICE LINE DO NOT

| emergency exit

chert | alarmed

POLICE LINE DO NOT CROSS POLICE LINE DO NOT

INE DO NOT CROSS POLICE LINE DO NOT CROSS

BROTHERS IN CRAP

A man with a warrant out for his arrest was pulled over in Thailand and, in the heat of the moment, gave his brother's name and address. Sadly, he had forgotten that his brother was also wanted for a crime. Both were arrested – not an outstanding example of brotherly love.

PICTURE CREDITS

AP/Press Association: pp. 11, 135 (Dave Thomson) and 137 (Jessica Kourkounis).

iStockphoto.com: pp. 21 (Don Bayley), 23 (Anthony Boulton), 29 (dondesigns), 31 (Alexandr Makarov), 43 (A-Digit), 51 (Andy Green), 57 (Eliza Snow), 63 (Floortje), 65 (Otmar Winterleitner), 69 (NREY), 71 (AAR Studio), 73 (Peter Garbet), 77 (Catherine Lane), 79 (Kamo), 81 (James Brey), 83 (bubaone), 89 (tomch), 105 (bubaone), 109 (DNY59), 117 (Hocus Focus Studio), 125 (Oktay Ortakcioglu), 129 (Floortje), 131 (loveguli), 141 (DNY59), 147 (Adriana Berned), 149 (4X-image), 151 (clu), 155 (Floortje), 159 (DNY59), 177 (Skip O'Donnell), 182 (Oytun Karadayi), 185 (Marilyn Nieves), 189 (Simon Smith), 193 (bubaone), 195 (Yuriy Kirsanov), 197 (JoKMedia), 199 (spxChrome), 201 (Zmeel Photography), 203 (Michael Hoerichs), 207 (Felix Möckel), 209 (Steve Katz), 215 (Evgeny Bashta).

Dreamstime.com: pp. 13 (Alex12345), 15 (Yannaphoto), 17 (Shawn Hempel), 19 (Natallia Khlapushyna), 25 (18percentgrey), 27 (Arenacreative) , 33 (Vyesikov), 35 (Alexander Oshvintsev), 37 (Aleksangel), 39 (Jiri Vaclavek), 41 (Ilyaka), 45 (Nikolay Mamluke), 47 (Nobeastsofierce), 49 (Galina Samoylovich), 53 (Alhovik), 55 (Vedmed85), 59 (Mirko Milutinovic), 61 (Brenda Carson), 67 (Sarah2), 75 (Robert Wisdom), 85 (Bartoszzakrzewski), 87 (Christophe Testi), 91 (Bert Folsom), 93 (Zoom-zoom), 95 (Dibrova), 97 (Aida Ricciardiello), 99 (Ivonne Wierink), 101 (Sergioua), 103 (Kitchner Bain), 107 (Jakatics), 111 (Berlinfoto), 113 (Ljupco Smokovski), 115 (Ljupco Smokovski), 119 (Goce Risteski), 121 (Roman Milert), 123 (Arne9001), 127 (Kitchner Bain), 139 (Vicsa), 143 (Radub85), 145 (Micha Rosenwirth), 153 (Captainzz), 157 (Denys Prokofyev), 161 (Wisconsinart), 163 (Felinda), 165 (Iqoncept), 169 (Anikasalsera), 171 (Volodymyrkrasyuk), 173 (Petr Malyshev), 175 (Vladimir Voronin), 179 (Igor Dmitriev), 181 (Adeliepenguin), 187 (Jovani Carlo Gorospe), 191 (Adrian Stones), 205 (Penywise) 211 (Nicemonkey), 213 (Lcro77).